P9-CJW-572

AMERICA
IN PASSING

To my friends
Monroe Wheeler, Beaumont and Nancy Newhall,
and Lincoln Kirstein,
who during the war had the idea of
putting on an exhibition of my work under
the title "Posthumous".

H. C.-B.
July 1991

AMERICA IN PASSING

HENRI CARTIER-BRESSON

INTRODUCTION BY GILLES MORA
DESIGNED BY ROBERT DELPIRE

FOREWORD BY ARTHUR MILLER

THAMES AND HUDSON

Introduction translated from the French by
JACQUELINE TAYLOR

First Published in Great Britain in 1991
by Thames and Hudson Ltd, London
This paperback edition 1996

© 1991 by Henri Cartier-Bresson and Editions du Seuil, Paris
English translation © 1991 by Thames and Hudson Ltd, London,
and Little, Brown and Company, Boston
Foreword © 1991, 1996 by Arthur Miller

Any copy of this book issued by the publisher is sold subject
to the condition that it shall not by way of trade or otherwise
be lent, resold, hired out or otherwise circulated without the
publisher's prior consent in any form of binding or cover than
that in which it is published and without a similar condition
including these words being imposed on a subsequent purchaser

All Rights Reserved. No part of this publication may be
reproduced or transmitted in any form or by any means,
electronic or mechanical, including photocopy, recording
or any other information storage and retrieval system,
without prior permission in writing from the publisher

British Library Cataloguing-in-Publication Data

A catalogue record for this book is available
from the British Library

ISBN 0-500-27914-4

Printed and bound in Switzerland

Contents

Foreword

There was plenty of glitz in America in the Sixties and Seventies, yes and in the Forties, the era of these pictures, but clearly Cartier-Bresson was trying to get behind it to the substance of American society. And since his is fundamentally a tragic vision he reacted most feelingly to what in America he saw as related to its decay, its pain. The very horizon is often oppressive, jagged with junked cars, the detritus of the consumer culture, which after all is a culture of planned waste, engineered obsolescence. Whatever lasts is boring, what demands its own replacement energizes our imaginations. These are painfully ironical pictures of the United States before Reagan's 'It's morning in America' made it so difficult, if not impermissible, to take a straight look at real life on this continent.

Cartier-Bresson knows that America arrives first at the crossroads, we are rushing toward the future at which Europe arrives, too, but a bit later. Thus, at least one of the impulses driving these pictures is to prophecy and warn his own continent, and Russia, too, and China, all humankind - that the future is a pile of used-up, junked people and their hollow idols, their adored machines. Unless a humanistic spirit is rediscovered and propitiated with an ethical love of earth and our own all but forgotten nature and its fabulous possibilities. Unless humankind once again stands at the center of creation, exalted by something other than the production-consumption squirrel cage.

It may seem odd to associate the poetic with so strict and even angry a vision but no one can look at these pictures without experiencing a curious intensity of feeling, as though the edge of some immemorial and dangerous mystery had been brought closer, as though an outcry were pressing toward one's lips. They are pictures at the abyss.

There is the poetry of the vague and of the concrete and these images are of the latter kind. Even the most populated of them betray the hints of classic triangulation, of line leading the eye to a vibrant center. But methodology is really only artistic instinct rationalized; one has the feeling here of something much more. An artist has found a way to apply his whole culture to the exposure in images of a paradox - the wealthiest and in many ways most benign society in history which at the same time is so hard, so brutal toward itself, so packed with vitality and hope and yet so close to terminal despair. The instant at which he seeks to blink his shutter is when hope crosses despair and the one lights up the other. This is the clash that creates the pathos of his pictures. And he is driven toward this moment by a persistent faith which every lasting art contains somewhere in itself. Faith is working through these pictures, and that may be the hidden reason why they seem so ageless. We cannot live on bread alone, but here, exposed to the light, is the bread we have tried to live on.

Since the Seventies the United States has become a different culture. The urgency behind these pictures now seems archaic. We are tired of so much knowing, we want diversion. These images ask the inevitable questions - What is our next chapter? Where do we go from here? And can the new impulse, whatever its mode, come forth with such rooted beauty?

ARTHUR MILLER

From One Extreme to the Other

Once the decision had been taken to publish a selection of Henri Cartier-Bresson's American photographs in book form, I realized that I would have to spend a good part of the winter of 1989-90 checking through his contact prints stored in Paris. I had just returned from a short visit to New York and I wanted to retain for as long as possible the proud, special light of October in Central Park.

Of course, my excitement about the project led me to overlook its real importance: hundreds of photos taken on his own account or for Magnum between 1946 and the end of the 1970s. It was a fascinating prospect. There would be America, there would be Cartier-Bresson — and there would be me, looking at both of them. When you think about it, I was really fortunate. I wouldn't have missed it for anything.

At the beginning of each week I would fly to Paris from Agen, taking the first morning departure. From Orly Airport I took the Métro to Place Saint-Michel. I liked to walk down the Rue Saint-André-des-Arts because this street has a store selling flying jackets. Nothing brought back the nostalgia of my childhood dreams of America more than those expensive leather garments, exact copies of the kind worn by US Navy pilots in World War II. I had bought mine in Atlanta, Georgia, in 1986. I was very proud of it, all the more so since one evening Jerry Lee Lewis had spilled bourbon all over it in the course of a boozing session. I noticed that the leather aged without cracking, a sure sign of quality.

At the Magnum offices I always got the floors mixed up and would go to the wrong door. Henri's contact prints occupied a whole stack of shelves. The first task was to decide on my priorities, to get myself organized. I decided to stick to a chronological approach and make a preliminary choice, wide-ranging and subjective. Then we would see.

Henri warned me, sensibly, "You're going to ruin your eyesight looking at those prints. You'll need to use the big magnifying glass. I'll call them and have them get it ready."

Everyone at Magnum knew about Henri's magnifying glass, but no-one was sure how to operate it. I hated the idea of having to use it. I prefer to look directly at photographs, with nothing between me and them. But this time I took his advice, knowing it made sense.

It was an awkward, uncomfortable piece of optical apparatus, made in Switzerland: a big lens was lit from below by a circular neon-light mounted on a metal support. At first the light flickered painfully and refused to function properly, so I had to fix up a hinged desk-lamp instead, directing the beam sideways onto the contact print. I found this complication intensely irritating, however, and almost began to blame Henri. In the end I told him about it, and next week I found the magnifying glass in perfect working order.

I spent the winter months studying his American pictures, mostly alone. Every now and then, one of the Magnum photographers, surprised to find me there, would lean over my shoulder to see what I was looking at. I would murmur mysteriously: "It's Henri's America," and the passing photographer would nod his head knowingly and leave me in peace.

I remember that, as I went through Henri's contact prints, I cheered him on aloud, as if reliving the moment when the image took shape in the viewfinder and feeling the need to celebrate each successful shot. Or I would take advantage of his absence to mutter a reprimand. Sometimes I came across images that made little impression; his eye had passed wearily over the American scene, abandoning any attempt to find a particular point of interest. In this dullness of vision, so untypical of Henri, I could recognize the same sense of frustration and strangeness which I had felt and which can make life in America hard for a foreigner to bear once he passes a certain threshold of familiarity.

Most often, however, I came across shots that were successful and found my mood brightening in sympathy. I sang out loud. At such moments I might call him at his studio. He hated that. He liked to spend each afternoon drawing. But I couldn't help myself, I had to share my discoveries. When he picked up the phone I would feel stupid, stammering some trite excuse, no longer confident that he would understand my elation. He had probably forgotten the pictures and the circumstances in which they were taken. Perhaps it even bored him to think about them again. I didn't want to force

him to take that trip into the past. The thing I enjoyed most about Henri was his total lack of nostalgia, his positive way of approaching the present, not letting himself be weighed down by that brilliant photographic career into which people tried, unsuccessfully, to corral him, when he himself had long since moved on to other things.

However, I felt it was only natural, when looking at his photographs, to want to look beyond the simple visual images and discover the stories that lay behind them. Yet with Henri that would have been pointless as well as useless, so when I saw him in the evening I hardly ever asked him for background anecdotes. He was grateful for that. I respected that mysterious side of his work which no doubt some academic would in due course probe relentlessly in the interests of biography. Henri's photographs in themselves were enough to evoke all the wealth of encounters and experiences that he carried within him. And I could not suppress a feeling of childlike wonder on learning that he had talked to William Faulkner, had sat at Marilyn Monroe's table or taken part in Kennedy's presidential campaign. I found these things absolutely mind-blowing, as if Henri, engaged in reporting the facts, had focused in himself the mythology of an America that I still dreamed about, that his pictures unfolded to me like some great picaresque tale.

One day, among photos he had taken on a trip to California via the South accompanied by the writer John Malcolm Brinnin, I recognized some buildings near Natchez, Mississippi, where I myself had stayed thirty years later. It pleased me to think that he too had been struck by the same scenes. Being familiar with the South, I responded more strongly to the pictures Henri had taken there. He and Truman Capote had visited New Orleans together. Capote, as I learned later, had followed Henri around in the heat, dragged along by the walking, inquisitive European through the lush, heavy greenery of the old trees until, exhausted, he turned his perpetual teenager's face, almost lost in the cool shade of a wistaria, towards the lens of the Leica.

Because of all this, I quickly realized that for me, over and above professional and critical interest, Henri's America would be a personal, almost private, thing. With the revelation that each of his contact prints brought, I was struck once again by the extent to which, in photography, the spectator's experience resembles that of someone reading a text. From one volume to the next, running like a thread through objective reporting as well as the most personal images, I now found an indefinable romantic quality which Cartier-Bresson's photographs had rarely held for me at first sight, viewed out of context.

Now these same images, in the light of the reality they revealed, seemed to me to lack the kind of visual geometry that Henri usually imposed on his shots. I discovered people, most of them anonymous, a few of them famous. I grasped situations. I recognized mythical places. Above all, I sensed a period whose measure he had taken more fully than he could have realized or intended, often intensified by an almost cinematographic chiaroscuro.

Comparing these American images with work I knew by other photographers, I was forced, after making allowances for differences in choice of subject or point of view, to recognize something they had in common that persisted like a sustained muted undertone, as if America were resisting each individual's personal language to transcend all of them, asserting the integrity of its culture and its territory. Even if Henri's images were marked by a distinctive "color", an indefinably European critical sense, a formal elegance, there remained an America consisting of intangible signs, architectural or geographical characteristics to which Cartier-Bresson, Walker Evans, Albert Stieglitz or Robert Frank had all had to submit, as if to a basic reality too strong to escape. Things that American photographers took in their stride, accepting them without question, had been for the European Cartier-Bresson a source of endless astonishment as his culture, vision, and tastes obstinately refused to accept the facts of American technology on which he was to depend for several years to come.

When the choice of photos had been made and the book had at last begun to take shape, Henri said to me, "Now it's your turn — go ahead and write!"

It was the end of May 1990, and there I was holding the baby, about to leave for the United States, where I would have to stay several months preparing a book and an exhibition on Walker Evans.

Unknown to Henri, the previous winter spent studying his pictures had greatly modified my views on photography, above all on his. The raw material of our book would be governed by that other great law of photographic choice, the editing process. On that subject Henri was intransigent. I had never felt so frustrated dealing with a photographer's work. Yet I knew that in any case many of the images I had selected would have to fall by the wayside. As the weeks went by, I had perniciously taken over his photographs, to the point where it seemed to me that the whole affair was not only about his America but a little bit about mine as well. After spending so long poring over Henri's American photographs, I had almost pushed him aside to replace him with my eyes, my story. When we came to reconcile the selections we had each made and assemble a final choice to make this book, I had the strange impression of a battle and a rescue. After it was all over and the photographs had been restored to their creator, I felt vaguely troubled by this conflict, as if I had been guilty of an unlawful abuse of his property. Of course I never told him so.

After all this, it seemed to me that for a long time to come I would be unable to think or write about other people's photography. I felt a lack of critical distance or, if you like, an excessive involvement of a kind other than what was needed for me to write an objective text.

I spent June getting ready for my visit, without really thinking about ideas for the text and how it might turn out. It would be about America, about photography, perhaps about Cartier-Bresson. On the last point I wasn't too sure. He himself encouraged me in this, wanting me to forget about him so as to express myself more freely about the rest. I was glad to know that it was his wish to see me retain an independent role in this joint project.

I remember taking leave of him in the Rue Jacob one lovely spring morning. I liked the way he dressed. That day he was wearing a neck scarf pinned with an American Indian brooch that matched his belt-buckle, the kind of articles you can pick up in the markets at Taos or Santa Fe, New Mexico. I said, "You look like a real Tex-Mex from the West!" He laughed. It occurred to me that, by the time I saw him again on my return from the United States, I would have completed the text, but at that very moment I had absolutely no idea how to tackle it. In both our minds, however, the book was already finished. It was as if we had spent all winter on an exhausting, adventurous expedition and were all set now to enjoy the freedom that followed. I looked at him, slim and lively, with his buckskin jacket and that Mexican peasant scarf. Impulsively I embraced him before leaving, happy to think of the time we had spent together, even if we had occasionally argued over details. In such cases we agreed to disagree, but on the essentials we were pretty much of one mind.

I spent a studious, boring July in New Haven, Connecticut. To be honest, I would have preferred to be in Spain or Italy. For me New England held few attractions. Still, the Yale fellowship had brought me here with my family, and I had to complete the Walker Evans job.

New Haven is like all the other cities of the East Coast: its age and maturity compensate to some extent for the depressing mediocrity of the suburbs. The center survives and Yale University, a mass of architecture more heavy than majestic, adds a restraining note of intellectual respectability. Yet everything is a stylistic muddle, ranging from Tudor neo-gothic to concrete avant-garde. On the far horizon your eye comes up against red basalt cliffs topped with dense vegetation.

We stayed in a handsome white timber house belonging to an academic, and situated at the bottom of the avenue that leads up to Yale. The owner had gone off to Maine to catch salmon, leaving me the run of his library, one of the best anywhere on the East Coast. I liked the house, probably because it looked like the ones Edward Hopper used to paint in the 1930s. It had two storeys and the typical gables of New England architecture. The garden, planted with birches and little firs, had a huge, immaculate lawn on which we played croquet in the evenings. I didn't have the worry of looking after it;

each week the gardener would come and trim the grass to the last fraction of an inch. Most importantly, the building extended into a porch providing a shady refuge from the heat. But we had to be careful — a big apple tree shed its fruit at the least breath of wind, threatening to fall on anyone below. Inside the house a system of steep, complicated staircases led up to the attic with its well-lit, practical study-library. Sometimes my son would relieve his boredom by strumming on the piano in the living room, always the same tune. The wrong notes were audible upstairs, half stifled by the heavy heat of the late afternoon.

The big problem for us was managing the alarm system. Every opening door or window, every blind corner of the living room or the bedrooms, was protected by electronic sensors which, in the event of an intrusion, activated a deafening siren, followed two minutes later by the arrival of police cars, for the whole system was linked to the local police station. There was a secret code which enabled you to override the system. We had the disagreeable sensation of living in a bank. Before going to bed at night we had to activate the alarm system, at the express desire of the owner. From then on we were trapped in our rooms, knowing that any attempt to go out, the slightest careless movement, might bring all hell down on our heads. We made that mistake twice, and twice the siren howled horrendously. Hopping mad, I chased all over the house looking for the magic code that would stop the alarm. Another night the neighbor's siren started up at full blast. We all stood in our rooms looking out as police cars surrounded the house. I went downstairs. A cop, gun in hand, was coming out of the window opposite. He had found nothing out of place. He was sweating, looking vaguely annoyed. "False alarm", he told me. "Their microwave must have triggered the system. We're used to it." In all this there was a hint of neurosis, not really worrying, more amusing.

Because of its configuration — you couldn't see the sea — and the continental heat, we found it hard to accept the fact that New Haven is a seaport. One day, however, we discovered the nearby beaches and were surprised to find girls in swimsuits, an ice-cream vendor, a man hiring out sunshades and beach-chairs. The sand, though fine, was too chalky for our taste. The presence of Long Island, with its peninsula stretching as far as the Massachusetts coast, tempered the force of the ocean waves. The undertow was weak, the water almost too cold despite it being the height of summer, so different from the South Carolina beaches we had encountered three years earlier. Yet over all this hung a sense of disrupted order that governed America and its ways, a hint of sensuality that appealed to us. Henri's photos of Coney Island had given me the same sensation. However, my interest in the beach soon faded. I was left with what I had come for: Evans's contact prints and the photography books on the library shelves. In the end,

fatigued by boredom and the heat, I immersed myself in them.

It was then that I found myself looking as if for the first time at America in photographs — taken by Paul Strand, Alfred Stieglitz, Edward Weston, Berenice Abbott, Ansel Adams, and so many others. I took careful notes. I thought about Henri. I noted the differences, took account of the similarities. I thought hard about this unprecedented photographic imagery. No country had ever been so worked over in images or so made its impact on those images, to the extent that for the first time I clearly grasped this truth: for me, for us Europeans, America was just *one* big photograph. As I amused myself by pursuing this thought to various conclusions, I found myself thinking more and more about the South, about Memphis, where I would once again be headed in a few weeks' time.

I had to put all these ideas in order, so as to shape them into an essay and thereby clarify them. But I was reluctant to start, already aware that the gesture was futile. This approach to photography was clearly just as simplistic as those already adopted by other photographers faced with the complex reality of America.

Yet here I was looking at the photos taken by Edward Weston for his Guggenheim Fellowship (1937-8: *American West*). The only image that moved me was a picture of a dead man in the Colorado desert. The others seemed tarnished, like so many photographic sediments deposited one on top of the other. Was it my own idle state of mind? I was struck as never before by the profound boredom of these images in which the mineral and the vegetable were raised to the rank of spectacle. Was it the enervating heat? I could no longer admire this same Weston's illustrations to Whitman's *Leaves of Grass,* for which in 1941 he had covered twenty thousand miles in ten months, met my old friend Clarence Laughlin in New Orleans, and ended his travels on the coast of Maine. Worse was to come. Paul Strand's *Time in New England,* for which I had felt some earlier liking, fell from my hands. I was sick of the studied frontality of these portraits, the affected gentility of all these homes, this over-lit vegetation. The images were there to underscore the message of the book, summed up in its dedication: "To the spirit of New England, which lives in all that is free, noble and courageous in America." I, a European fed on surrealism, a notorious skeptic, am suspicious of this photographic enthusiasm for order and purity underlined by natural materials — the timber of the churches, the celebration of human types, all lined up there to make you believe in a predestination of objective forms. I won't have it: this purpose is alien to photography which should not define essentials, but convey a moment, a touch, a mood. Looking at these pictures, I found myself regretting the absence of chance and the unexpected in so much American photography, which is more often inclined to stop and calculate, grasp at coincidences, always ready to pounce on the essence, the symbol.

Very serious now, I jotted down the outlines of an essay on a sheet of paper:

The Photographic Americas:

- those photographed in the spirit of American documentary (from the nineteenth-century landscapists to Robert Adams and Lewis Baltz, via Evans...)
- those photographed by foreigners, Europeans (Frank, Cartier-Bresson...)
- what we know of America through photography. Those who teach us more about photography than about America (Stieglitz, Weston, Gibson...) The opposite (the Farm Security Administration). Those who do both (Evans, Friedlander...)
- the cinema, American photography: the great agitation of our visual (un)conscious. Can the myth still work? Isn't it saturated, even exhausted?

I wrote and wrote. When evening came, I would go out into New Haven Green to listen to the open-air concerts. For me the most enjoyable was Tito Puente's band playing Latin American rhythms. The smell of patchouli and spicy picnics filled the air around the Puerto Ricans in the audience. Children let their balloons float up into the sky, where the crescent moon shone. Two solitary clouds, very low and colored pink by the artificial light below, hung softly over the park, indifferent to the salsas the band was playing. Behind us black women were dancing with each other. Others were clinging lovingly to their men. All that writing I had done during the day seemed quite unimportant.

Once a week I went to New York. Sometimes I took the train. It was the only way to enter by degrees, as one should arrive in a real city. The train made its way through decrepit, ill-defined, deserted suburbs bypassed by the freeways. Sometimes the train would stop briefly and then start up again with a great clatter. Blurred by motion, the graffiti on the walls formed an indecipherable frieze like a decorative ribbon. Beyond the curves and between the buildings I could glimpse, always with the same delighted surprise, the Manhattan skyline with its many skyscrapers.

The city sweltered in the stifling summer heat and looked dirtier than ever. About noon a thunderstorm might break, washing away the filth in the streets with a warm deluge. Caught in the rain one day, I ran into St Thomas's Church on Fifth Avenue. I was seized by the chill within, accompanied by an overpowering odor of disinfectant. Two or three great stained-glass windows, the same shade of blue as Hollywood swimming pools, slyly allowed a little warmth into the solemn atmosphere. Although it promotes God wholeheartedly, America, I noticed not for the first time, does not get along well with holy things.

I spent most of any time in New York scouring the archives of the Museum of Modern Art. One day, as I looked through some documents, I came across an invitation card:

Documentary and Antigraphic Photographs by Cartier-Bresson, Walker Evans and Alvarez Bravo.
April 23-May 7 1935.
Julian Levy Gallery, 602 Madison Avenue, New York.

Opening my notebook, I carefully copied the calligraphic ornament that decorated the card. Two eyes stared back at me, amused no doubt by the message they were sending me. Henri and Walker, to both of whom I was so close, together on the walls of a New York art gallery in the 1930s... A chance discovery was giving me a structure for my idea of America. I went out almost at once, feeling the urge to rediscover right away the face of New York as it had been then, just as they must have found it in 1935, to the astonishment of Henri, who had just arrived from Mexico. No doubt he had booked himself a passage from Vera Cruz to New York on some ramshackle old steamer. No doubt he would have in his head still, and for a long time to come, the exotic wild craziness of towns in Mexico which he had just witnessed.

So on landing in New York, arriving for the first time in North America, a place he had previously only imagined from the movies of his adolescence, from reading an old guide-book inherited from his father or from Melville's novels, he came face to face with another world, another kind of craziness, perhaps too well-behaved or too pragmatic to interest him visually at first. For a whole year, he told me, he forgot his camera; instead he would while away the time watching movies or wandering the streets of Harlem or the East Side. A photograph by Hoyningen-Huene taken at about the same time seemed to me for some inexplicable reason to reveal the hunger he felt to live life at first hand.

I came out of the museum and walked as far as the Chrysler Building. Then I took a taxi past Radio City, all the way up to Harlem and the Apollo Theater. Coming back down, halfway along Broadway I noticed the Hotel Martinique, deserted now but with its blue and black sign still intact after nearly fifty years, taking its place alongside that other landmark of the past, the invitation card I had chanced upon in the Museum of Modern Art.

> "But where would it be this time? The names of cities called to him — Memphis, Wilmington, Gastonia, New Orleans. He would go somewhere. But not out of the South... He did not long for open space and freedom — just the reverse."
>
> Carson McCullers
> (*The Heart Is a Lonely Hunter*)

Soon we had to quit the New Haven house when the owner returned. My wife and son went back to France and I stayed on alone. As usual, I headed for the South, where I had no particular plans except to attend a commemoration of Elvis Presley with Carl Perkins in Memphis. Until then I would travel around. Before taking the plane, I called William C. He had been actively recording the Alabama scene for at least thirty years.

"Bill," I said, "I'll come and join you in Tuscaloosa, and Alabama here we come!"

He was jubilant, knowing I was almost more crazy about the South than he was. The first time we met, I had astonished him by describing, house by house, the route between Moundville and Greensboro, Alabama, where he had spent his childhood. Apart from Lee Friedlander, I was the only person he had ever allowed to tag along, to be introduced to his damned photographic paradise, Hale County, full of drought and rednecks.

The weeks spent in New England had reassured me about some basic things. First, America had never seemed to me to be so much itself as in places well away from big cities. It had to be as far away as possible from the present for me to be able to rediscover the myths it held for me through its music and literature and through photographs. I didn't want to lose any more time. The South meant all this to me and I had to check that it was still there.

So when I drove out of Memphis in mid-afternoon en route to Oxford, Mississippi, I became aware almost at once of the obvious differences from the other America that I had left behind in the rain that morning. There were not many cars about, and they were nearly all big, old, and battered, in shades of yellow and green. A truck overtook me. I had time to see the faces of the driver and passenger, dirty, haggard, imbued with violence and with that threatening, uncivilized quality that New England has almost succeeded in erasing. How else do you explain the rifle hung in the rear window? And then the swamp vegetation, growing like a skin over the abandoned homes under the kazoos, homes quite without style, stuck out there away from any neighborhood — what for, for Heaven's sake?

On the way out of Holly Springs, where I stopped to drink a Coke at the nickel-plated drugstore counter (fast disappearing in the East), there was a warning to drivers:

"Buckle up, it's the law!"

A nice example of American discipline, complying without protest, without fuss... This was also something to worry a libertarian like Henri Cartier-Bresson, so profoundly attached to Montesquieu's dictum: "Laws are necessary relationships derived from the nature of things."

I had backed a loser: in Oxford the swimming pool at my usual motel was unusable, due to a blocked pipe. Since leaving New Haven, I had been looking forward to its coolness, picturing myself after a swim, sitting in the shade and starting work on the text to accompany Henri's photos. I had sent him a postcard, lying shamelessly, saying that the preparation was proceeding well. And now I had to figure out another situation, another place to write in. I had come to Oxford partly for that swimming pool and for the pleasure of the little town that my memory, playing tricks, had transformed into a summer resort.

Greatly put out, I went out to the square with its monument to the Confederate Soldier and into Square Books, a quite well stocked café-bookstore. Oxford was actually becoming a fashionable intellectual center, rather like Santa Fe in New Mexico. In the bookstore I found several copies of my own book on Walker Evans next to Henri's publications, with a portrait of William Faulkner, taken by Henri right here in Oxford thirty years before, framed and hung on the wall beside them. Once again I decided to trust to luck and see how things turned out. Most important of all, my eye was caught by an open balcony overlooking the square and the street, on the upper floor of the bookstore. You could take a seat there, and order an iced tea. I had just found the perfect replacement for my swimming pool.

I stayed a few days in Oxford, in no hurry to write, preferring to take photographs. I always found some excuse, some place to visit. At high noon I crossed the town on foot as far as Rowan Oak. No doubt I was hoping to find a dog preparing to stretch itself out on Faulkner's departed shadow. At most I found the blinding sunlight and the incessant sound of the crickets. A tree lay across the grass in front of the stables, seeming to bar the way to them.

In the evenings, on the bookstore balcony, I browsed and watched the black kids going past on their skateboards. I hadn't brought many books along with me: two or three Dashiell Hammetts, a 1930s guide to Mississippi, and Baudrillard's *L'Amérique.* I re-read the last one cautiously, as if its text might have used up all that I myself had to say about America. So what did I have to say about it, in fact? Why was it that, faced with America in particular, I had to adopt the attitude and the viewpoint of a fascinated anthropologist? If America still held any surprises for a European, they were slowly being reduced to tired old myths which no longer existed for Americans. Baudrillard had been right when he wrote: "It may be that the truth about America cannot be seen by a European for himself."

Ever since de Tocqueville in the nineteenth century, this question of cultural distance had of course provided the chief fuel of the great machines churning out talk about America that I was so sick of. I myself responded to lighter touches which only reached me more strongly and truly through certain photographs, the flavor of old movies or my adolescent infatuation with Elvis's music. I found it easier to believe in the truth of our childhood America, with its wide-open spaces for the imagination. The map of these, never definitive, was proving inexhaustible beyond the prosaic and often disappointing reality, even if seeking it out cost me endless effort.

I reached Alabama in two days. Ignoring the freeways and taking the state highways instead, I stuck to the itinerary recommended by my 1930s guidebook, getting a real kick out of checking the details it provided, finding some hamlet still almost intact, with its crossroads and gas station miraculously unchanged. Only somebody who has traveled through Mississippi in this unhurried, attentive way can claim to *know* America. He must stop his car at noon on Main Street (Aberdeen, Mississippi), return the unwelcoming, suspicious stares of the regulars at the only open diner in the place, and order the day's special. After the meal, he must take a short walk on the shady side of Main Street, to the steady hum of air-conditioners, to explore the local bazaar with its jumble of bric-à-brac, so different from the meticulous tidiness of the department stores. These big, orderly stores I rediscovered at night in the malls, those great air-conditioned cathedrals of commerce. The shopping mall is like a covered city with streets, fountains, empty restaurant terraces. In modern America the malls have taken the place of downtown centers which are now abandoned to the blacks and their poverty.

Thanks to the malls, uniformity reigns all over the United States, undermining traditions, taking over the street scene, killing the very idea of the pedestrian. The South held out a little longer, sure, but in every little town the corner grocery has been replaced by the supermarket, the drugstore by McDonald's, Heartbreak Hotel by a national hotel chain, and now all is enclosed in the mall, accessible only via the parking lot.

Order. Duplication. The Same Again. A succession of monotonous façades that America has used through the years to cover up, shuddering with distaste, its landscape and its way of life. Side by side with this process, the element of surprise was disappearing. I was astonished by this every time I visited the United States, and it left me wondering how long it would be before I finally forsook America out of sheer boredom. This alone meant that from now on, whatever my destination, each new stay in America would sum up in itself, without gain or loss, the essence of all the previous ones. The experience was no longer cumulative. Trying to remember each visit, I always ended up by turning to the last, as if the earlier ones had been canceled out by being too like each other.

I left Columbus, Mississippi, as always, in a state of frustration, despairing of finding a way to express its charms in photographic terms, when faced with the stereotypes it offered me: whiter-than-white colonial homes, cemeteries softened by the shade of cypresses, a general degeneration of people and things. American picturesqueness (here, I could feel it) seemed to me like a standard selection of photographic clichés thumbed through many times over. Deep down I was annoyed with myself for all these markers that I had set up between my eyes and America, so spoiling it for me.

I pulled up in front of a signboard at the door of a rather beautiful house. It was Tennessee Williams's birthplace. This surprised me for I had always thought he came from Louisiana. As I was preparing to photograph the house, a little black girl popped up, just to my left, in her white Sunday dress. When she saw me, she stuck out her tongue and ran off, holding the hem of her dress, perfectly reproducing an image Henri had captured in New Orleans forty-five years earlier — an unexpected bonus.

Henri had deliberately turned his back on the American landscape, preferring the human scene in accordance with his inclination and his culture. Turning everything around, he had made up his mind to Europeanize America and built it photographically around its people — their gestures and the meaning of their gestures. For Cartier-Bresson America was a complex and profoundly human stage on which a play rich in meaning was presented and he had to elbow his way to the front so as to enjoy the best moments to the full, ignoring the uninteresting ones.

Just the opposite was true of Evans, Friedlander or Winogrand. In their photographs I became aware of the absence of any particular drama and of a consequently heightened interest in the backdrop. Nature, culture, characteristics and people were all flattened out against it in a jumble, in no particular order of importance, with no meaningful depth that could serve as a basis for a point of view to hold up against others and develop into a moral or, worse still, a philosophy of humanism. As I saw it, for many of its own photographers America meant above all a chance to capture more or less attractive visual moments which an impatient European might easily judge too harshly on account of an apparent lack of differentiation.

I received some confirmation of all this when I met my friend, the photographer Bill C., in Tuscaloosa, Alabama. We were to travel together again through Hale County, a decaying corner of Alabama where in 1936 Walker Evans and James Agee had conceived their celebrated book *Let Us Now Praise Famous Men.* I had already been there more than once, trying to rediscover the essence of a nostalgia whose origin, apart from the lasting wonder of Agee's text and Evans's images, still puzzled me as much as ever. Why, in the whole of the United States, where I had traveled extensively, did I have to pick for my dream spot this desolate stretch of wooded hills, red earth littered with dilapidated buildings and erupting into three or four sleepy little townships so backward in outlook that I could not contemplate without a sense of terror the thought of staying there more than three days? Bill was born here. Later he moved to Washington, D.C., but returned every summer to see his family and to register on film the inexorable decline of his native county, systematically photographing everything that would soon disappear from the scene forever.

That morning, when Bill and I set out very early to make the most of the daylight, the light still had a warm glow. The road toward Moundville and Greensboro follows the green line of the kazoos, drawn like a phantom horizon. Bill had carefully coordinated his itinerary, holding on his lap the pictures taken a year earlier of this or that building soon to disappear, each of which he methodically re-shot in color, using a clumsy large-format camera. At the end of a red earth track stood a cylindrical tower, pink like Toulouse brick. With touching pride Bill informed me that it dated from before the Civil War (the "antebellum" tag is the most prestigious guarantee of respectable antiquity). A little later he stopped in wonder, as if before a great work of art, at an inscription clumsily painted on a board. "Hand-made," he explained to me, underlining its artistic value. (Incidentally, Bill removes these various signs indicating make and origin and preserves them to display alongside his photographs.) At some point during the three days we spent together I too started looking out for rusty old thermometers nailed to garage doors, half-erased advertisements for chewing tobacco, or simply the thousand subtle variations on the Coca-Cola label that Pop Art had been exploiting for thirty years.

Somewhere before Greensboro we photographed an old cotton warehouse. Bill was fascinated by the delicate patchwork of brown tones caused by the rusting of the metal surfaces. "It's beautiful," he said, not thinking for a second that I might find the epithet surprising. I am always amazed at the low standard applied to beauty in America, even though I can understand the attraction to the vernacular which Bill shares with a number of American artists. How could I tell him without shocking him that my interest lay elsewhere? Nonetheless, in this rockbottom of the human spirit which is Hale County, each of us was finding his home ground: he, because he was born and reborn there, the latter photographically; I, because on every trip there I lived joyfully through a small death.

America, I could feel it, was getting us all going, each for his own reasons. Mine, at bottom, were pretty feeble ones, firmly rooted in my teenage dreams.

For a long time I had let myself believe in love's delusions. I loved America and hoped it would return my affection. When I was living there (in Jena, Louisiana, with its 2500 inhabitants), I already had problems putting up with its caprices. Because I found it hard to share the country's faith, its enthusiasms and its inhibitions, America looked at me askance. We didn't go to church — people turned their backs on us. Back in the 1970s, I wore my hair long and sported an arrogant moustache — I had to cut them short. For some months I hated America for making me go around half bald. Its answer to my anger was always the same, sticking to shop windows and on the windscreens of cars:

"America, love it or leave it!"

Worse: while I found a million excuses for sensual delights in the South, America was set on preventing me from enjoying them. If we fancied a beer, we had to drive miles to buy it (Jena itself was "dry"). I bought *Penthouse* under the counter, furtively pointing to where the newsvendor had it tucked away to combat galloping obscenity. And on my driver's license, no doubt to avoid any misunderstanding, care was taken to specify that I was white.

In winter I would go out with other Frenchmen hunting wild pig with bows and arrows. Then we barbecued them, basted with bourbon. It was not strictly legal. But all the time I was living there, I had a feeling that my romance with America could easily turn sour. Love it or leave it! No half measures, no flabby compromise, no semantic excuse of the "and/or" variety. Couldn't you, for example, imagine leaving it while still loving it? Or leaving it *because* you loved it? In America emotions tend to be oversimplified, which makes them worrying.

I left America almost hating it. Returning to it later from the cultural angle of its photography, I began to love it again but in a more rational way, which is a kind of end to the affair. So began a kind of *pas de deux* which went on for a long time. From a distance I dreamed about America through its images, and more and more through its music. Then, when I was actually there, I sought perfect harmony — America *and* its images — though I knew all along that such an ambition was a vain hope. So while I kept up the pretense, I became less trusting (more clearsighted perhaps?) I would certainly have to give

America the brush-off one of these days, break off the relationship altogether. I didn't see it as a bitter parting of the ways, but rather as an amicable separation, of which I was already having a foretaste of during this visit.

However, when I left Tuscaloosa and headed for Memphis again through the slumber of the deep South, I was feeling pretty cheerful.

"Memphis!," I said aloud, alone in my Chevrolet. And, as always, I could clearly envision the scaly façades of the movie theaters on Lamar Boulevard, the big empty white home of that other Southern photographer, William Eggleston, the way night fell suddenly on the town, and the symbolic yellow sun of Sun Studios (706 Union Street), where the rock'n'roll music of Elvis Presley and my friend Carl Perkins was born.

Big Carl and I were to meet there for the closing concert of the annual Elvis Presley commemoration held every August to mark the anniversary of his death. I too was there on a pilgrimage. I laughed to myself. I had come over to the United States to do research on the work of Walker Evans, then got involved in the exacting task of composing a text to accompany photographs by Henri Cartier-Bresson, and now here I was at the gates of Memphis, guitar in hand, ready to do reverence to the King, the ex-truck driver from Tupelo, Mississippi. And I knew I was going to have a great time.

It has taken me a long time to grasp one simple, irrational fact: that beyond my interest in American culture, the country's real attraction for me was rock'n'roll. I could have chosen another, more noble musical genre. Jazz had a far higher prestige value — it could keep step with the avant-garde, take its place in the spiritual epic of America, break through the barriers of segregation, seduce Stravinsky and Scott Fitzgerald, adapt itself to Cubism, to the lyrical vistas of abstract expressionism, to the machine-made poetry of the Beat Generation or even to the folklore of Sartrean existentialism. Jazz, which bridged the generation gap and was taught in universities in between two courses in "creative writing," carried the illusions of modernism to their highest point and finally succeeded in re-tying the two loose ends of America: its congenital primitivism and its wily sophistication.

But Elvis? Rock'n'roll, faithful to its tacky origins, to its cut-price world, had found in Presley its incarnation in an equally cut-price myth without any intellectual stature, a myth that never became an esthetic to be rediscovered (except by show business); a myth to which the deep South clung with the good sense of a people fully aware of the realities of their situation. For me rock'n'roll still meant the excitement of a kind of music in which (though I hate having to give this explanation, so out of keeping with its subject) the *performance* was as important, if not more so, than the *statement* (musically speaking). From the moment of its birth in the 1950s rock had relied on outward appearances, as hollow, futile and wretched as the frustrated environment that brought it forth, the world of disc-jockeys and pink Cadillacs. Jazz has never been kitsch. Rock'n'roll and the deep South are basically just that, as much as Elvis's own Grace-land a few blocks away in Memphis, where I was due to go later that day to meet up with Carl Perkins, one of the first heroes of this flashy mythology.

I had first met Perkins a few years earlier with Jerry Lee Lewis in Atlanta, Georgia. Both of them were pushing fifty, bent on eternalizing the rebellious spirit of rock'n'roll, for they were its only remaining exponents now that Elvis was dead. I do not believe Carl had ever appreciated the true depth of my passion for his music. In his eyes I was a slightly deviant foreign intellectual, a seeker after the exotic, crazy enough to come down to his level by singing along with him. Not long afterwards, I managed to arrange for him to come and perform with me in France, at an open-air concert in the Roman theater in Arles in early summer. Overcome with wonder, he had whispered to me like a shy child: "Oh God! I've never played in such a beautiful place." And all the other performers from Nashville and Memphis, Tennessee, who for thirty years had been pounding out their music in such places as the casinos of Las Vegas and the nightclubs of Miami, experienced something of the radiant solemnity of that extraordinary night.

Now, a year later, I met Carl Perkins once again, this time on his own ground at the heart of the myths which he epitomized. At five o'clock we were settling the band into the hall of the Airport Sheraton. That evening the closing concert of the annual Elvis Presley commemoration would bring together Elvis's daughter, his old friends, musicians, benefactors and beneficiaries of the Presley Foundation.

But in the midst of my joy at being reunited with Carl and his band, I looked around at the place and was amazed at the meanness of this impersonal setting — low ceilings, depressing tables, lighting better suited to some shady joint, a few miserable portraits of Elvis hung haphazardly around the walls. At eight o'clock they all came in together and took their places: a procession of pale faces, heavy silhouettes, elderly women with their hair piled into elaborate beehives. Elvis's songs, played at low volume over loudspeakers, competed with the muffled voices. At first I failed to recognize them. It was as if their charm obstinately refused to operate. I could hear only a faint, simple rhythm where normally Elvis's voice — and Carl's — transfused these insignificant tunes with a primordial rush of vital energy in which I, at forty-five, could still find the illusion of eternal adolescence.

Someone pointed out Elvis's daughter, sitting at the high table: I saw a drab figure of a young woman, somewhat overweight, surrounded by stiff-backed sexagenarians. On the stage a local MC introduced, though without conviction, Presley's former cronies who had come along to trot out their well-worn anecdotes. People laughed in moderation, taking care not to make too much noise. They were already feeling bored.

I recognized Elvis's earliest musicians, whom I had admired devotedly for years. Carl introduced them to me. They went on stage to try to recapture the old magic of their music. I was appalled: a few sad contortions reduced the rebellious rock'n'roll music to a clapped-out machine without soul or excitement. Behind them, on a giant video screen and apparently oblivious of them, Elvis, filmed live on stage at twenty, swung his hips, his guitar and his frenzy as if in the realm of silent movies. Then the sound system snorted harshly. It provided a handy signal for the interval.

I took a few photos, shook the hand of Elvis's ex-drummer, a great gangling guy from Shreveport, Louisiana, and went back with him to rejoin Carl Perkins and his group before following him onto the stage feeling as emotional as a child. Once again I forgot everything else as I listened to that voice, to which I occasionally added my own, rushing to catch up with those twanging bursts of electric guitar music and recapture for a few minutes the delight that a few moments earlier I had thought was lost forever. Elvis was undeniably dead. Thanks to the tameness of the show put on to celebrate his memory by people who had actually known him, and in spite of Carl's talent, I felt my America slipping away as surely as, throughout this trip, I had a feeling of impending catastrophe. As soon as the concert was over, I left Carl to his admirers. I wanted to be alone, to escape from Memphis, which felt like a trap.

So I retrieved my car and drove away, skirting the airport and passing through the black sections of town. People were sitting out on the steps in front of their wooden verandahs, not giving a damn about Elvis and his admirers. I drove carefully, looking out for kids who might run across the street without warning. Some of them would shake their fists at me. Then I was back in the countryside and on the road to Natchez, and after passing the last motel, I was on the highway to Tupelo. I parked the Chevrolet and switched off the ignition. At once I found myself in the noisy night of the Old South with its incessant buzz of insects.

I lay down on the ground with my back against the edge of the ditch. I let the usual string of images run through my mind. Then, in order to banish the evening's events from my thoughts, I tried to recall the course of the route as far as Nashville, the woods it passed through, the sandy creeks that you would never suspect were to be found under the masses of arching vegetation. Under the American night I imagined the way ahead, the real countryside well away from towns, freeways and airports, as far as the threshold of Virginia and beyond it to Bangor, Maine.

There I lay with a river at my back. It flowed silently by like some moving walkway.

I could only tell it was there by the degree of humidity and the constant drips all around me. I adapted my breathing to the still night air. Close to my face a firefly gleamed. I picked it up delicately and put it on the viewfinder of the Leica, where it made a little yellow flickering glow. I gently turned the camera up to the starry sky and looked at it through the viewfinder, lit by the insect, which I then put gently back on the ground.

Suddenly, reminded no doubt by the Leica, I thought of Henri. And a fact struck me, blindingly: throughout all his encounters, his reporting, among the extraordinary list of celebrities, events and myths which he had chronicled on his numerous trips to America, Henri Cartier-Bresson had never taken a picture of Elvis Presley!

Completely alone, I laughed out loud at my discovery, which I am sure the history of photography will not hold against me. Whatever may have been the reasons, trivial or profound, for this omission, I said to myself that in any case I was there for the purpose of recording it.

Then I must have fallen asleep for a few minutes. Very soon I was woken again by distant sounds of motors and voices. Suddenly I felt scared. Closing the Chevrolet door with a bang, I got back on the road in the troubled uncertainty of dawn.

Gilles MORA
October 1990

NEW YORK, 1959 / NEW YORK, 1947 ▷

NEW YORK, 1947 / NEW YORK, 1959

DETROIT, 1947 / MIAMI, 1956

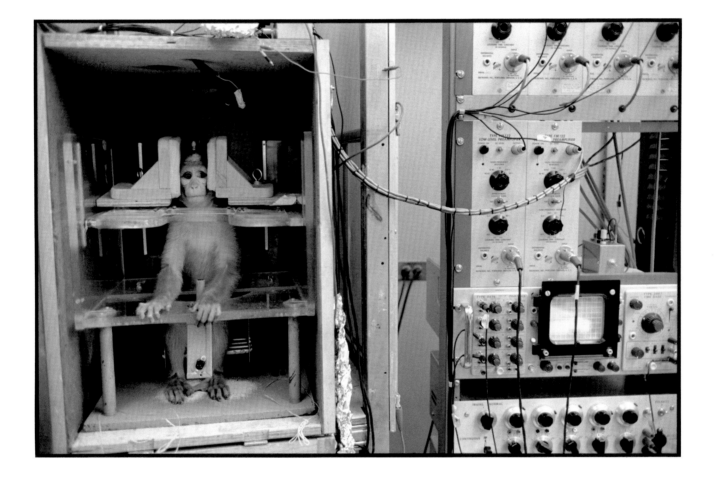

FLORIDA, 1968 / BERKELEY, 1968

NEW YORK, 1961

NEW YORK, 1957 / LOS ANGELES, 1947

Hoffman, Bevin Talk Over Crisis

Eden Is Gloomy On Nation's Plight

Laborite Government's Policies Deplored by Ex-Foreign Minister

By Ned Russell

LONDON, Aug. 24 — Paul G. Hoffman, Economic Cooperation Administrator, discussed the dollar crisis of Britain and the sterling area today with Foreign Secretary Ernest Bevin, Harold Wilson, President of the Board of Trade, and other British officials.

Mr. Hoffman's discussions today began a three-day series of talks which are expected to embrace the whole problem of the dollar-sterling area to find a way of balancing their trade with the United States.

The talks are being conducted virtually on the eve of the Washington conference, beginning September 7 in London, when British and Canadian foreign and finance Ministers on the crucial question of obtaining an equilibrium in trade between the United States and Canada...

Mickman Swims the Channel, In Water for Almost 24 Hours

Philip Mickman, eighteen-year-old British schoolboy, who swam the English Channel yesterday in the longest time on record—23 hours and 48 minutes.

British Schoolboy, 18, Was Carried 14 Miles by Cross-Tide, But Refused to Give Up

DOVER, England, Aug. 24 — Philip Mickman, eighteen-year-old British schoolboy...

Tito Denies Joining Plot On Albania

Asserts He Wants No Part of Territory

Rejects Albanian Protest On Frontier Violations, Jabs at the Cominform

By the Associated Press

BELGRADE, Aug. 24 — Yugoslavia officially denied tonight any part in a supposed plot to carve up Albania under an agreement by which it would acquire part of the territory...

Cominform Is Securing Its Borders

Tightens Barriers In Anti-Tito Drive

West Allies Get Reports Of Fortifications From Baltic to the Near East

By Marguerite Higgins

BERLIN, Aug. 24 — The Soviet orbit in Europe, from the Baltic Sea to the Near East, has in recent months intensified security measures...

Atlantic Pact Is As Truman Pl 12 Nations' Acc

Armed Services to Cut 147,000 From Pay Rolls Immediately

Reductions Will Include Some 12,000 Reserve Officers to Be Returned to an Inactive Status

WASHINGTON, Aug. 24 — Secretary of Defense Louis Johnson announced today that the armed services will shed 147,000 civilian employees from their pay rolls and return more than 12,000 reserve officers to an inactive status...

Chiang's Regime Flees Chengtu and Sets Up Its Capital on Formosa

U.S., Britain, France Are Due To Recognize Mao Shortly

Paris Diplomatic Sources Say Such Action Is Possible Within a Matter of Weeks

Armies Under Hu Are Left Behind

2 Guerrilla Commands To Be Directed From The Capital of Sikang

TUC Council Approves Report

Warning of Levies on Business

Tough Language Tells British Labor Only Harder Work Will Improve Standards

By Jack Tait

LONDON, Aug. 24 — Britain's trade union leadership approved today a special report which tells the nation's 8,000,000 workers in tough language that business is being taxed already to the limit and that their only hope for an improved standard of living is to work harder.

Edited and Published in Europe

New York Herald Tribune

Edition

63d Year—No. 20,806

PARIS, SATURDAY, DECEMBER 17, 1949

U.S. Offers Bank Plan For Europe

Would Establish A Clearing House

U.S. Is Reported to Feel Scheme Is Important As Integration Move

By Kenyon Kilbon

The United States is pressing the western European countries with a plan for establishment of a European central bank, it was learned yesterday.

Up in Central Park

Debate Set On Budget In France

Radical-Socialists Yield to Bidault

Assembly to Get Project Monday; 20-Billion-Fr. Hole Must Be Filled

By William J. Humphreys

Will Leave State Dept.

Jessip to Quit State Dept. Post

Kostov Dies After Plea Is Rejected

Goes to Gallows In Treason Case

Presidium of Assembly Decides Not to Grant Appeal for Clemency

By the United Press

FRANKFURT, Dec. 16 — Traicho Kostov, condemned to death for treason and espionage by the Bulgarian Supreme Court Wednesday, was hanged today after his plea for clemency was rejected by the Presidium of the National Assembly, the official Bulgarian agency reported as monitored here...

Mao in M Praises Of Soviet

Russians Cut Off Power To Berlin's West Zones

is in other goods shipments. Whether the Soviets need Ruhr coal enough to lift their blockade remains at this point doubtful.

The excuse for the latest phase of the Soviet campaign against the Western Allies was the announcement that the west deutschmark would be introduced in the city The American-sponsored currency will rival the new Russian-stamped mark in the east sector. The Russian mark is also in force in the Soviet Zone.

Russian Argument

The Russians argue that Berlin must be absorbed in their zone because the Western Allies by setting up a western German state have lost all right to remain in this four-power city.

Population Fears Slow Starvation

Cut of Food, Coal Trains from the West Brings Biggest Post-War Crisis

By Marguerite Higgins
From the Herald Tribune Bureau
BERLIN, June 24.—Soviet economic warfare against the Western Allies and the German population of Berlin reached an unprecedented intensity today, precipitating Europe's greatest post-war crisis.

Russian power cuts plunged much of western Berlin into darkness for as a continued Soviet blockade of the German population cut off from food and coal supplies and even orders even stopped delivery of fresh milk, endangering health of German.

Starvation As Weapon

Actual starvation of the population of western Berlin is probably the only weapon that might bring success to the Russian drive to oust the Western Allies from Berlin, according to well-informed quarters.

The potentially explosive Berlin situation developed quickly tonight. During the evening 100 British and Russian troops, in full battle-dress, took up positions facing each other at a border point of their respective occupation sectors. The quarrel resulted from a Soviet attempt to seize the goods of a scrap merchant of the British sector whose yard is located near the Soviet sector When German police got cold feet, British troops were sent along to give them moral support.

In all four sectors of the city German police were alerted.

Throughout the day, American armored cars patrolled the streets of the American-occupied sector. The Germans found them a reassuring sight.

lin in its fight for independence."

This afternoon the British, in retaliation for the Soviet blockade of Berlin, cut off all coal and steel deliveries to the Soviet Zone as well.

Clay Holds Only Act of War Could Drive U.S. Out of Berlin

Says No Soviet Pressure Will Halt Projects of Allies in Western Zones

By Edwin Hartrich
From the Herald Tribune
FRANKFURT

off electricity and rail traffic into the beleaguered city as "the strongest pressure that has yet been applied to push us out of Berlin."

No Soviet pressure tactics nor any new eastern German government that might be created by the Russians will halt the British

General Lucius D. Clay

SUNDAY, JUNE 27, 1948

West Sets Up Air Supply Line To Feed Its Sectors of Berlin; New Mark Cuts Currency 90%

'Zones' Economy Down to Bedrock

By Edwin Hartrich
From the Herald Tribune Bureau
FRANKFURT, June 26.—At midnight tonight 90% of the monetary value of western Germany will be wiped out by a decree of the American, British and French Military Governors. Promulgation of a conversion law of one new west German deutschmark for ten old

Churchill Supports Laborites In Decision to Stay in Berlin

Tells Conservative Party That Firm and Resolute Course Is Only Way to Ward Off Dangers; Assails Government's Policy in India

From the Herald Tribune Bureau
LONDON, June 26.—Winston Churchill told a Conservative party rally this evening that the Berlin crisis "raises issues as grave as know were at stake

have said Britain intends to stay in Berlin "without having made sure that the United States were equally resolved." There is no guaranty that "even a firm and resolute course will ward off dangers which

Planes Will Defer Ebbing of Supplies

By Marguerite Higgins
From the Herald Tribune Bureau
BERLIN, June 26.—The British, with American support, demanded today that the Russians lift the blockade that threatens hunger for the German population in the western sectors of Berlin.

This first official Western Allied protest to the Soviet military administration came as plans were being completed for the inauguration on Monday of an unexpectedly extensive air supply service to bring food to Germans in Berlin.

The air supply armada that will tax the facilities of the air fields

CAPE COD, MASSACHUSETTS, 1947 / WASHINGTON, D.C., 1958 ▷

NEW YORK, 1959 / NEW YORK, 1946

NEW YORK, 1960

ILLINOIS, 1961 / NEW YORK, 1957

WASHINGTON, D.C., 1957 / NEW YORK, 1947

NEW JERSEY, 1975 / WASHINGTON, D.C., 1957

NEW YORK, 1947 / ANN ARBOR, MICHIGAN, 1960

LINCOLN, NEBRASKA, 1956 / TEXAS, 1947

MILWAUKEE, WISCONSIN, 1957 / ANN ARBOR, MICHIGAN, 1960

es Not Intend
Call Congress

London Awa
Invasion Ne

By Gaston Coblentz

LONDON Oct. 31 — Britain and France launched their assault against Egypt late this afternoon with the aim of recapturing the Suez Canal Zone.

Invaders

gary's
Deal
erging

ently Free;
ion Seen

Israeli troops advancing under cover of a smokescreen in Egyptian territory

In Washington

Politicians Feel C...
Will S...

Yucel

FRIDAY, APRIL 6, 1951

2 Atom Spies Get Death;
3d Sentenced to 30 Year

Execution in May
For Rosenbergs

1st U.S. Citizens Ever to
Get Supreme Penalty
On Charge Seem Calm

By Blaine Littell

From the Herald Tribune Bureau
Copyright 1951 New York Herald Tribune, Inc.

NEW YORK, April 5 — Julius and Ethel Rosenberg were sentenced to death today for the part they played in a Soviet espionage ring which stole atomic secrets from this country in World War II.

ral Part of
ngle of Wr

Whites Bar Six Negro Pupils
from North Little Rock School

Governor Stands by Decision

Situation Is Quiet At Central High

By the Associated Press

LITTLE ROCK, Ark., Sept 9.—White students threw back six Negro youth who tried to enter North Little Rock High School today as the first

chool, which opened today for the fall term.

The six Negroes tried a second time to enter when school superintendent F. B. Wright came out of the school building and gestured to them to follow him in.

But as the Negroes climbed the steps again, reinforcements, including adults, ran to the support of the white students. An estimated 1,500 persons surged around the Negroes.

Mr. Wright gave up and told four Negro adults who accompanied the Negro students to meet him at a downtown office later.

Police made no effort to escort the Negroes inside the building. Their only action was to breach the first

FRIDAY, MARCH 19, 1954

OCTOBER 10, 1951

hate Group Moves to Open vestigation on Sen. McCarthy

By Don Irwin

On the Herald Tribune Bureau and New York Herald Tribune, Inc.

SHINGTON, Oct. 9.— The e elections subcommittee took first step today toward possible n on the resolution by Sen. am Benton, D., Conn., calling an investigation as to whether Joseph R. McCarthy, R., Wis. ho be expelled from the Senate.

an Guy M. Gillette, chairman, reporters the five-member committee had directed its to report back by Nov. 1 with dings of fact on the ten rged against Sen. McCarthy ced Sept. 28 by Sen. Benton.

r. Gillette said his group would eet at that time to decide on ther action.

Sen. Gillette also showed report a letter from Sen. McCarthy clining to appear to answer the charges. He said the subcommittee ook no action on another letter rom Sen. Benton urging that the .... anded into the period

that the Senate employ its little-used expulsion machinery against Sen. McCarthy on the general charge that the Wisconsin Republican had used "calculated deceit and falsehood" both in his campaign against alleged Communists in the State Department and in other phases of his Senate career.

The general charge was supported by ten "cases" in which Sen. Benton undertook to show that Sen. McCarthy had committed "perjury" in some phases of his campaign and had deceived the Senate in others.

Sen. McCarthy's letter to Sen. Gillette, dated Oct. 4 reiterated the counter-charge of Communist ties with which he has thus far met Sen. Benton's accusations.

"Frankly, Guy," the letter said in part, "I have not and do not intend to even read, much less answer, Sen. Benton's smear attack. I am sure you realize the Benton type of material can be found in the Daily Worker almost any day of the week and will continue to youths and pens

Criticism of Methods
Spurned by McCarthy

By Homer Bigart

Special to the Herald Tribune
Copyright New York Herald Tribune, Inc.

CHICAGO, March 18.— Sen. Joseph R. McCarthy, R., Wis., said here last night he would continue to fight Communists with his own particular methods, regardless of whether any official liked those methods or not.

"I don't give a tinker's dam how high or how low are the people in either the Republican or Democratic parties who are unhappy about our methods," Sen. McCarthy told 1,200 persons at a St. Patrick's Day dinner of the Irish Fellowship Club.

"This fight will go on as long as I am in the United States Senate," he said. Mr. McCarthy is chairman of the Senate Permanent Investigations subcommittee.

Opening a Mid-West speaking tour, Sen. McCarthy intimated that the Eisenhower administration was being taken in by the Communist line.

At an earlier press conference McCarthy dismiss-

dent Eisenhower's backing of Secretary of the Army Robert T. Stevens in a test of veracity between himself and Mr. Stevens.

Presidents always support members of their official families, he said, adding, "the President reacted as he would have to do with any Cabinet member."

Sen. McCarthy said he would "back to the hilt" Roy M. Cohn who has been charged by the Army with trying to pressure into giving preferential treatment to Pvt. G. David Schine, former unpaid consultant to the McCarthy subcommittee. Sen. McCarthy and Mr. Cohn have charged Secretary Stevens and Army Counselor John G. Adams with trying to "blackmail" them into calling off further investigations of alleged subversion in the Army.

Greeted with cries of "Give them hell, Joe!" and "You're in your own ballpark!" Sen. McCarthy likened his methods to those employed by St. Patrick.

"The snakes didn't like St. Patrick's methods," he said, "and the Communists don't like

NEW YORK, 1947

BOSTON, 1947 / DETROIT, 1947

HOBOKEN, NEW JERSEY, 1947

LOUISIANA, 1958 / TENNESSEE, 1946

NEW YORK, 1945 / CHICAGO, 1945

NEW YORK, 1935 / MISSISSIPPI, 1962

HARLEM, 1947 / IOWA, 1947

NEW YORK, 1959 / CHICAGO, 1947

HARLEM, 1947 / LOS ANGELES, 1947

NEW YORK, 1946 / RICHMOND, VIRGINIA, 1960

NEW YORK, 1959 / RENO, NEVADA, 1947

WASHINGTON, D.C., 1958 / NEW YORK, 1959

RENO, NEVADA, 1961 / MASSACHUSETTS, 1947

Tells Police 'I Did It for Jacqueline;' President's Body Borne to Capitol

Accused Assassin Killed During Prison Transfer

DALLAS, Nov. 24—Lee Harvey Oswald, the accused assassin of President Kennedy, was himself shot and killed here today while being transferred under heavy guard from one prison to another. He was shot down at pointblank range by a man identified by police as 50-year-old striptease-club-owner Jack Ruby, and died two hours later.

Police said Ruby told them he shot Oswald because of a deep sense of feeling for Mrs. Jacqueline Kennedy, the President's widow. He added that he wanted to spare her the ordeal of the trial of the accused killer.

Police quoted him as saying "I didn't want to be a hero. I did it for Jacqueline Kennedy."

Oswald was rushed to the same hospital in which President Kennedy died but despite an emergency operation, blood transfusions and heart massage he died at 1.07 p.m. two days and seven minutes after the.....

Case Against Oswald Airtight, Police Say

DALLAS, Nov. 24—Police said today they had an airtight case against Lee Harvey Oswald, the accused slayer of President Kennedy, before he himself was shot.

The evidence against him included a photograph of him holding what was alleged to be the $5 Carcano bolt action rifle that the assassin fired at Mr. Kennedy from the fifth story of a downtown Dallas building.

The photograph also showed him holding what was alleged to be the pistol used to shoot and kill pursuing Patrolman J.D. Tippit shortly after the assassination of the President.

But even when presented with the photographs and other incriminating evidence, the 24-year-old ex-marine and self-proclaimed Marxist steadfastly maintained his innocence and denied killing either man.

Case Clinched

Despite his refusal to make confession, homicide chief Will Fritz said: "This case is cinched. The man killed President Kennedy. We are convinced without any doubt he did the killing," Capt. Fritz said.

It was the shooting of Patrolman Tippit about four miles from where President Kennedy was shot that gave police the break in their hunt for the President's assassin.

This was how......... of Oswald's movements.

He was spotted by a Texas Book Depository policeman searching from where he....... fired.

Oswald was still in building a snack he drank in his hand.

Mr. Truly said that no significance on Oswald......

Gov. Connally Told of Death Of Kennedy

DALLAS, Nov. 24—Texas Gov. John Connally, out of danger and recovering satisfactorily from an assassin's bullet, learned from his wife yesterday that his personal friend, President Kennedy, is dead.

Mrs. Connally talked to the Texas Governor shortly after 7 a.m. and his first question was about the President's condition.

After hearing her answer, he said "That's what I was afraid of."

Gov. Connally, Mr. Kennedy's Navy Secretary before he resigned to run for Governor last year, was riding with Mr. Kennedy when the bullets struck.

He remained conscious after the shooting until he was put under heavy sedation. He raised slightly Friday night but was unable to ask the question. It was his first question on waking Saturday.

President Shot First

When the shots were fired the Governor was sitting in a jump seat of the big Presidential limousine opposite the President. His wife Nellie was sitting on the jump seat next to Mrs. Kennedy.

The President was shot first and sheriff's deputies who heard the shots said there was a pause of several seconds before two more shots followed.

To that shot that the Governor reacted in bewilderment to turn toward the slumping President.....

'I Knew What

By B.H. ......
DALLAS, Nov. 24—AP)—A.....

Case Against Oswald

Cabinet Officers to Stay On

WASHINGTON, Nov. 24—The wheels of American government almost brought to a standstill by the tragic slaying of John F. Kennedy, have been set rolling again by a resolute President Lyndon B. Johnson.

In one of his first major acts as President, he asked the members of the Kennedy Cabinet yesterday to stay on to serve him, and got their pledge to remain as long as he wants them. From members of Congress he received assurances of bipartisan support.

Round of Conferences

To all the ambassadors and chiefs of mission abroad he sent a message asking them to stay on the job and not submit the usual resignations.

As rain drenched the grief-stricken city, the new President drove himself through a busy day of conferences with government leaders and former Presidents' aides to the nation and made plans to address the Congress next Wednesday.

A high Administration official in disclosing earlier that Mr. Johnson would address Congress, said "I do not expect it to be a program speech or a partisan speech."

The address is expected to be an appeal for unity. It was noted that Harry S. Truman brought such an appeal to Congress on April 16, 1945, only four days after Franklin D. Roosevelt's death made Mr. Truman President. The nation then was engaged in World War II.

Today, among many other activities Mr. Johnson received an intelligence briefing from John A. McCone, director of the Central Intelligence Agency, and McGeorge Bundy, Presidential Special Assistant for National Security, and discussed the situation in South Vietnam with Ambassador Henry Cabot Lodge, Secretary of State Dean Rusk and Defense Secretary Robert S. McNamara.

Attends Rites

He also attended services for the late President in St. Mark's Episcopal Church and participated in the procession bringing Mr. Kennedy's body to the Capitol.

Yesterday, he found time to call on Mrs. Jacqueline Kennedy and to attend with Mrs. Johnson a brief special service at St. John's Episcopal Church. And the 36th President issued a proclamation designating tomorrow as a national day of mourning for Mr. Kennedy.

Except for three brief trips, Mr. Johnson spent little time in the White House where his quarters on until this afternoon was temporary in a suite in the majestic Old East Room.

Mr. Johnson worked from his old suite in the Executive Office Building across the street. There around a little table in front of the desk he has been using since he moved in as Vice President in January 1961, he conferred with Congressional leaders and Cabinet officials.

Ex-Presidents Call

To give what help they could he also summoned the bodies of office former President Dwight D. Eisenhower and Mr. Truman called on Mr. Johnson.

The two former American Presidents also visited the White House to pay their respects to Mr. Kennedy.

An aura of grief pervaded Mr. Johnson's office as the conference shuttled in and out.

Mr. Johnson started his first full day as President at 8:45 a.m. An early morning drizzle had temporarily ended it quickened later.....

END OF AN ASSASSIN—Jack Ruby, Dallas nightclub owner, aims pistol at Lee Oswald, suspected slayer of President Kennedy, at the Dallas City Jail yesterday. An instant later, Ruby fired, fatally wounding Lee Oswald in the stomach.

Kennedy Children Procession

To the muffled beat of drums, Kennedy's body was today borne in stage from the White House in final homage of a grieving nation ten and 12 deep as the crowds lined the sun-swept streets.

Mrs. Jacqueline Kennedy, dressed in black, a veil drawn back from her pale, tired, face, rode behind the gun carriage with her children, Caroline, six, and John, whose third birthday is tomorrow.

Riderless Horse

In a tradition going back to an ancient military ceremonial, the nation's fallen Commander-in-Chief was also followed by a riderless charger with boots reversed in the stirrups as a sign of mourning, behind a lone sailor bearing the President's personal standard and a pallbearer detail drawn from all branches of the services, came members of the immediate family and President Lyndon B. Johnson, travelling in a fleet of slow-moving limousines.

The solemn procession wound its way up to the top of Capitol Hill as an Air Force band played flourishes and flourishes, and "Hail to the Chief"—which, in life, greeted the President on his first appearance at public functions.

Same as Lincoln

The casket was carried into the rotunda of the Capitol to lie in state on the same catafalque that bore the last remains of another assassinated President—Abraham Lincoln—nearly a century ago. It lay immediately beneath the Capitol's 180-foot-high rotunda, flanked by national and Presidential standards.

After the coffin was in place, Chief Justice Earl Warren made a tearful and moving plea for an end to "the bitterness that begets violence."

"Surely there is a lesson to be learned from this tragic event," he said.

"If we really love this country; if we truly love justice and mercy and if we fervently want to make the tomorrow a better for those who are to follow us, we can at least abjure the hatred that consumes people, the false accusations that divide us and the bitterness that begets violence," he said.

When the Presidential wreath had been put in place, Mrs. Kennedy moved forward hand-in-hand with Caroline along the coffin. Touching the flag, she knelt beside it and kissed it. Caroline also touched the flag and paused momentarily while her mother bowed her head. Then both stood and walked back to their places.

Then the mourners stepped out of the Capitol. President Johnson and his

Continued on Page 2, Col. 6)

Observe Silence In Mourning

During the President's.....

New York the Metropolitan and Broadway theatres have.....

Kennedy Says Se......

Nehru Asks To Halt

NEW DELHI, Oct. 22—Prime Minister Jawaharlal Nehru today called on the people of India to put their enemy on a war footing to meet Communist Chinese aggression.

In a nationwide radio address, the 73-year-old Prime Minister warned that Chinese troops had invaded India's disputed northeast and northwestern frontiers and were facing the situation in three areas.

"If we want to save our freedom," Nehru said, "we must change our processes, our ways of thinking, and move in a way which greatly increases our production," he said.

Detective Saw Ruby

'I Knew What

Open to West

BERLIN, Aug. 13 - The East German r...
the Communist bloc, closed the East W...
border early this morning.

East German armed forces occupied
threatened to shoot angry anti-Communi...
reopening of their escape route to the We...

Thousands of East German soldiers po...
militia with Soviet tanks in
reserve stood in a city that
could explode into open revolt.

Ader
Says
Will

Radio
Beamed

NEW YORK Herald Tribune

European Edition

PARIS, TUESDAY, OCTOBER 23, 1962

Largest circulation of any American newspaper published

Price Per Copy

rders Blockade on Weapons for Cuba
t Missile Sites There Peril America

Guantanamo Base To Be Reinforced

Peking Bid To Join UN Is Debated

Formosa Raps Attack on India

UNITED NATIONS, N.Y., Oct. 22 - Nationalist China called for rejection of the Soviet Union's annual bid to seat Communist China in the United Nations General Assembly as soon as it was made today.

WASHINGTON, Oct. 22 - President Kennedy declared tonight that the United States will stop and turn back any ship carrying weapons of an offensive nature to Cuba.

He announced this blockade of Cuba after stating he had unmistakable evidence that the Soviet Union had begun to build missile sites there capable of raining destruction on the Americas.

Dobrynin Silent at Briefing

r Economy hina Threat

Court Says Judge

DAY OF CRISIS - President Kennedy between meetings on the Cuba crisis at the White House, yesterday.

VERMONT, 1960

LYNCHBURG, VIRGINIA, 1947 / ARIZONA, 1947

TENNESSEE, 1947 / OXFORD, MISSISSIPPI, 1947

VICKSBURG, MISSISSIPPI, 1947 / SOUTH CAROLINA, 1960

CHICAGO, 1947 / HARLEM, 1947

NEW YORK, 1946 / NATCHEZ, MISSISSIPPI, 1947

ROAD CLOSED
TO THRU TRAFFIC

TEXAS, 1956 / VERMONT, 1960

LOS ANGELES, 1947

ASPEN, COLORADO, 1971 / SARATOGA, NEW YORK, 1947

NEW YORK, 1959 / LOS ANGELES, 1947

...dy Calls Feat ...portant Step'

...April 12 — President John F. Kennedy...

3 Astronauts Of U.S. Use Same Word

All Are 'Disappointed' At Not Orbiting First

LANGLEY AIR FORCE BASE, Va., April 12. (AP) — ...pointed...

America's three leading astronauts used identical expressions in...

Space Race Began Over Decade Ago

But First Sputnik Gave It Impetus

From the Herald Tribune Bureau

NEW YORK, April 12 — The race into space has been a cold-war battle for supremacy between United States and Russian scientists for more than a decade.

It began obscurely, but grew into prominence with the launching of Russia's Sputnik I on Oct. 4, 1957. And now the Russians have demonstrated again their ability to perform the spectacular with the orbiting of the first man in space.

Hybrid Rocket

A significant day in the history of the United States program came on Feb. 24, 1949, from a flat desert relay in White Sands Proving Grounds, N.M., when a hybrid German-American rocket blasted 250 miles straight up to a point where the atmosphere is so thin that one molecule of air must travel five miles to collide with its nearest neighbor.

First Against

FIRST MAN IN SPACE — Maj. Yuri A. Gagarin.

Gagarin, 27, Was Born On a Collective Farm

From Cable Dispatches

MOSCOW, April 12 — His name means "wild duck."

It is pronounced Gah-gah-rin with the accent on the last syllable.

No Injury

His first words on returning to earth, according to Tass, the Soviet news agency, was:

"I am glad to tell the party, the government and Nikita Khrushchev personally that the landing was normal. I feel well. I have no bruises or injuries."

Space Firsts In Russia, U.S.

WASHINGTON, April 12 (UPI) — Following is a chronological summary of Soviet and United States space firsts and their launching dates:

Russia
First earth satellite, Sputnik I, Oct. 4, 1957.

Mercury Speed-Up Pondered

Pressure Likely For Early Effort

From the Herald Tribune Bureau

NEW YORK, April 12 — that the Soviets have launched a man into space, the United States program faces its most crucial test. Can the engineers and scientists of Project Mercury resist inevitable pressure in speed-up?

Is Watched on T... Says 'I Feel Fi...

From Cable Dispatches

MOSCOW, April 12 — The Soviet Union 27-year-old airman into orbit around the earth and him back safely to win the man-in-space race United States.

Premier Nikita S. Khrushchev hailed the as "an example of courage, gallantry and... streets of Moscow erupted into a demonstration...

M... Two Ast... Prepare...

By Al Rossiter Jr.

SPACE CENTER, Houston, July 20, 1969 (UPI) — Man landed on the moon today.

Two pioneers from the planet Earth, American astronauts Neil A. Armstrong and Edwin E. Aldrin, flew their fragile spacecraft to a braking but safe touchdown at 20:17:40 GMT.

'Quite a Lot of Rocks' at Site

...s Can't Atone, ...cial Prosecutor

French A-Test in December Not Full Technical Success

By Don Cook

PARIS, April 13 — The first French atomic test explosion in the Sahara...

U.S.-Wide Rallies Held Against Vietnam War

By United Press International

NEW YORK, March 27.—More than 50,000 anti-Vietnam war demonstrators paraded down Fifth Avenue all afternoon yesterday, pelted by eggs and an occasional fist, to cheer speakers at a Central Park rally.

Authorities said it was the largest pacifist demonstration ever held in the city, far surpassing the first antiwar rally held last October.

Marchers were still streaming into the park's gigantic mall, which was filled to over- three hours after the demon-

A crowd of about 500, mostly supporters of the veterans, watched the burnings. A few spectators hissed and heckled.

The second incident came before the parade yesterday when a Molotov cocktail was thrown at the office of one of the 70 participating organizations, the Committee Political Action.

strations, but no outbreaks were reported in yesterday's march.

Bystanders and leather-jacketed motorcyclists heckled 1,000 marchers as they plodded along a five-mile route from Cambridge Common into Boston. Before the march started and after it got under way, six motorcyclists drove their machines in and around the group, shouting epithets.

2,650 marchers in a peace parade. A score of young men walked along beside the head of the procession, shouting insults. There was a brief scuffle between hecklers and marchers.

Egg-throwing hecklers disrupted an antiwar rally in the city hall plaza of Worcester, Mass. There were two arrests.

In Cleveland, Ohio, about 350 to 400 college students staged a Vietnam protest march. There were about 25 counterpickets but no incidents.

More antiwar marches took place in Miami, Gainesville, Fla., Barabo, Wis., Kenosha, Wis., Los Angeles, Philadelphia, Houston, El Paso, Denver and other cities.

Minneapolis marchers were confronted by a picket carrying a sign which read: "I'd rather fight than switch."

Three persons were arrested by police breaking up fistfights between protestors and hecklers in Detroit's Kennedy Square when 30 members of "Break Through," a Conservative group, attacked marchers.

Violence broke out at Oklahoma City, where ten sign-carrying pickets marched shoulder-to-shoulder outside the federal building.

ON MOON
nauts Land Craft Safely
Walk on Surface Today

APOLLO 11

The cool spacemen called out their final figures as they dropped toward the lunar surface.

At 220 feet "Coming down nicely."

At 75 feet "Looking good."

At 30 feet "Picking up some dust."

Then, finally at 2017:40 GMT "Contact light. The Eagle has landed."

At the time of the landing the moon was about milt from earth. Michael Collins the third astronaut the Apollo 11 team kept the command ship orbiting the moon at an altitude of 65 miles while Armstrong and Col. Aldrin eased their way down.

Col. Collins was poised to swoop in and rescue his colleagues, had anything gone wrong, but now that are on the lunar surface, they are beyond his reach.

"Out the window is a relatively level plain cratered a thoroughly large number of craters of the variety and some small... 5 to 50 feet high and thousands of one and two-foot craters around the Mr. Armstrong said.

"We are some angular blocks several hundred front of us.

At her Houston home, Mrs. Aldrin stood up minutes before touchdown.

"When it came the just can't believe it."

Takes Control Manually

tors turned out in force—00 to 100,000—to protest for n Vietnam. In background, g a stop to Communism antiwar demonstrators carry ome of American fighting men.

PEACE IN VIETNAM

HELP! STOP WAR IN VIETNAM

GET U. OUT OF NO

NEW YORK, 1947 / NEW YORK, 1959 ▷

NEW YORK, 1947

NEW YORK, 1947

NEW YORK, 1947 / MEMPHIS, TENNESSEE, 1947

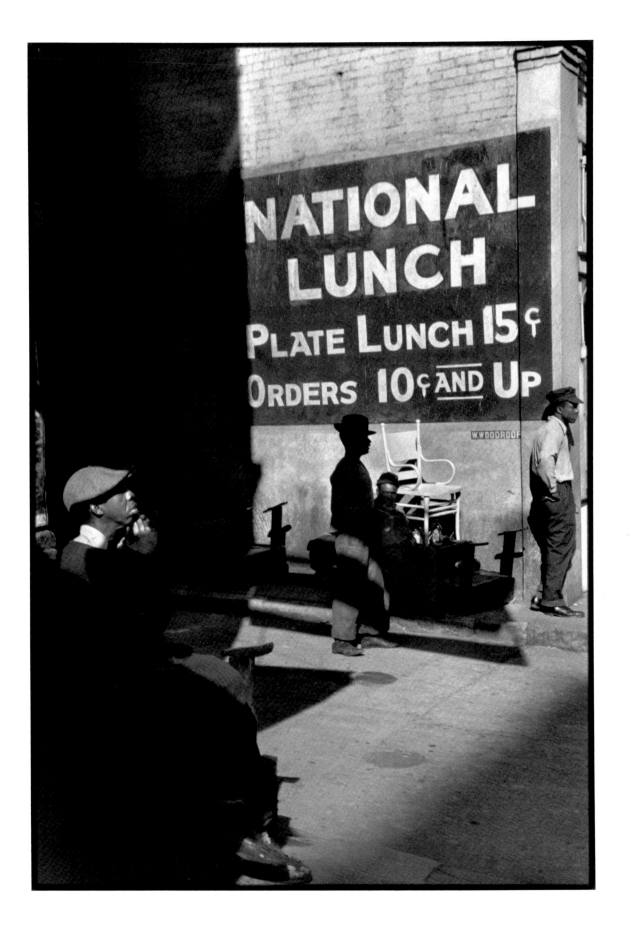

NEW YORK, 1947 / HARLEM, 1962

NEW YORK, 1947 / CHICAGO, 1947

Guard Commander Feels Firing Was Not Justified

KENT, Ohio, May 5 (Reuters).—Brig. Gen. Robert Canterbury said here today he felt that National Guardsmen under his command had not been justified in firing on a crowd of demonstrators at the Kent State University campus yesterday.

Gen. Canterbury, Assistant Adjutant General of the Ohio State National Guard, told a press conference that an investigation had found that 14 of about 100 Guardsmen had discharged a total of 35 rounds at the crowd, killing four of them and wounding nine others.

Asked if he thought the Guardsmen had been correct in firing on the demonstrators the general said: "In the light of the consequences, where four students lost their lives, it was not justified and could never be justified."

However, he stressed that the Guardsmen had fired because they feared for their lives.

"I was there, I was hit by rocks and I felt that I could have been killed," he said.

U.S. Campuses Seething, Day of Mourning Planned

By Robert Siner

WASHINGTON, May 5.—About 1,000 persons massed on the steps of the Capitol today to protest the U.S. invasion of Cambodia in a prelude to what may be the largest and most violent round of demonstrations against the Indochina war.

Anti-war groups called for rallies and vigils on Thursday, a national day of mourning Friday and a march on the White House Saturday.

The Capitol demonstrators were made up mostly of congressional aides and members of the League of Women Voters, which is holding a convention here.

Despite rejection of a demand that it suspend the Cambodia session, the League recessed its convention for the day so that about 600 of its 2,900 delegates could attend the protest.

Meanwhile, with peaceful strikes and violent marches, with flower-draped crosses, black arm bands and anti-war buttons; with firebombs, window smashing and stone throwing—American college students showed their sorrow and their rage at the widening of the war and the fatal shooting of four students in Ohio.

The Senate Democratic leader Mike Mansfield of Montana, commenting on the violence at Kent State University in Ohio and other campuses said: "I hope this doesn't mean the beginning but rather the end of situations of this kind."

Sen. Frank Moss, D-Utah, (Continued on Page 2, Col. 7)

surrounding communities, occupied the campus Friday to deal with anti-war demonstrators. Yesterday, during the noon hour, their routine occupation produced an American tragedy.

Facts Are Unknown

No one—neither students nor guardsmen nor university officials—could say precisely what happened. They all recite the same fragmentary story.

On the grassy commons behind the administration building, several hundred students massed to continue their protests against the war in Southeast Asia and against the presence of the guardsmen.

Hundreds of other students were on nearby slopes surrounding the commons. Other hundreds were leaving their classrooms, walking to lunch through the area.

Guardsmen, carrying loaded rifles with bayonets fixed, were lined up facing the students on the green. They stood with their backs to the charred shell of an ROTC building destroyed by incendiaries Saturday night.

An order to disperse was given over a bullhorn. It was in keeping with an edict by Ohio's Gov. James A. Rhodes banning all outdoor demonstrations on the campus.

The order was met by shouts, obscenities and stone-throwing from the crowd.

The helmeted troopers were ordered by Brig. Gen. Robert Canterbury to move on the crowd and disperse it. The troopers forced the students back, firing tear gas as they advanced. They were met with a barrage of stones and unexploded tear-gas canisters.

The guardsmen had driven the students over the crest of (Continued on Page 2, Col. 4)

Below, one of the participa is wrapped in an American At right, demonstrators swa with protester on top way the background is the dom

Nix

Will

WASHIN
ident Nix
the death
University
frontation
Guardsme
campus re
expression

The
prefaced b
pathy for
victims, w
House new
He later i

No. 27,154

Jeffrey G. Miller   Allison Krause   Sandy Lee Scheuer   William K. Schroede

Kent Coed's Epitaph: 'Flowers Are Better Than Bullets'

KENT, Ohio, May 5 (AP).—Allison Krause, a 19-year-old girl from Pittsburgh, frequently carried her pet kitten around the campus. She placed a flower in a National Guardsman's rifle last Sunday and said: "Flowers are better than bullets."

major and was serious about the causes of violence on campus.

Jeffrey G. Miller, 20, of Plainview, N.Y., was described by home-town high school friends as "studious, not rebellious, quiet and intelligent."

200,000 in Washington Anti-War Ma...

By James M. Naughton

WASHINGTON, April 25 (NYT) —Anti-war marchers massed yesterday at a new rallying point, the Capitol, to urge Congress to assume the leadership they seek to bring the Indochina war to an immediate end.

The huge crowd, predominantly young, was peaceful as it gathered behind the White House —the focal point of other peace rallies and strolled for three hours down Pennsylvania Avenue to the grounds of the Capitol

and women who were participating in a Quaker peace vigil at the White House, the Associated Press reported

[Seventy-nine women and 45 men were arrested for crossing police lines outside the presidential mansion where they had gone to voice disagreement with President Nixon's statement that he as a Quaker is seeking peace in Indochina

[The charge is a minor one, carrying a $25 fine]

"We would like," one speaker said "for the whole world to

...stood in massed groups outside the executive mansion.

The huge crowd at the Capitol was less electric in mood than the 70,000 to 100,000 protesters who streamed angrily to the Ellipse last May to protest the US incursion into Cambodia. But it was larger

It did not approach in numbers the 320,000 who gathered around the Washington Monument in November, 1969 —the largest anti-war demonstration ever—but it seemed to be slightly more representative of adult

---

Herald INTERNATIONAL Tribune

Published with The New York Times and The Washington Post

Established 1887

PARIS, WEDNESDAY, MAY 6, 1970

Nixon Tells Congress Leaders GIs Will Exit in 6 to 8 Weeks

State Dept. Calls It A 'Hope'

By Spencer Rich

WASHINGTON, May 5 (WP) —President Nixon told members of the Senate and House Armed Services Committee today at a closed briefing that he is firmly committed to withdrawing US troops from Cambodia before the monsoon rains start. The pullout was promised within six to eight weeks, the congressmen said.

But the State Department spokesman Robert J. McCloskey said it was the hope that the Cambodian action can be terminated in six to eight weeks. It was noted that the seminated in six to eight weeks. It was noted that the seminated into Cambodia...

BLAZING GUNS—Twin 50-calibre machine guns slash streaks of fire across the night sky as a personnel carrier crew battle a North Vietnamese ground attack in the Memot district of...

Airlifted U.S. and Saigon Troops
Open New Cambodian Operation

NEW YORK, 1947

SAN FRANCISCO, 1946 / HARLEM, 1947 / CHICAGO, 1947 ▷

RALEIGH, NORTH CAROLINA, 1960 / SAN ANTONIO, TEXAS, 1947

CAPE COD, MASSACHUSETTS, 1947 / GRAYLING, MICHIGAN, 1961

SAINT FRANCISVILLE, LOUISIANA, 1947 / HARLEM, 1947

TEXAS, 1958 / NEW YORK, 1947

NEW YORK, 1959

List of Illustrations

Acknowledgments

I should like to record in black and white my appreciation of the help provided by the following individuals and magazines, all of them instrumental in one way or another in aiding the creative process of taking the photographs which are reproduced in this book. My thanks go to: Pierre Bérès, John Malcolm Brinnin, Truman Capote, Norma Copley, Martine Franck, Alfred Kazin, Lincoln Kirstein, Sergio Larrain, Kate Lewin, Inge Morath, Dorothy Norman, Alan Porter, Pat Strathern, and Helen Wright; also to *Life, Harper's Bazaar, Paris-Match, Holiday,* and *Vogue.* Finally, I wish to thank Ideodis Création and Magnum Photos.

Paris, March 1991   H. C.-B.

Photocomposition, photolithography, and printing
by Entreprise d'arts graphiques Jean Genoud SA, Lausanne
Bound by Mayer et Soutter, Lausanne